You Think You Can Drive!

E. M. Williams

ISBN: 978-1-4834-1254-2 (sc)
ISBN: 978-1-4834-1253-5 (e)

Library of Congress Control Number: 2014908954

Lulu Publishing Services rev. date: 06/02/2014

PREFACE

Traveling the highways daily you become very observant of some of the strange behaviors that's placed on display by motorist. It make you give thought about other motorist state of mind. To bare witness to some of the activities that occur around you everyday give you a different view of why rules of the road should be followed. This book was written for those who will be more observant of bad driving behavior and drive more defensively.

EPIGRAPH

How can a man call himself a man when he neglects what is felt in the heart and soul? How can a man call himself a man when what he does and says is dictated by bonds of loyalty and not free thoughts? Absence of morals he can be called a man due to his physical attributes.

CONTENTS

YOU THINK YOU CAN DRIVE!

The alarm on your clock sounds with one of your favorite songs playing on the radio and you awaken to the brisk bite of the dampness of the room indicating a cold morning to start the day. Eyes not yet fully opened, you struggle with your feet to locate the slippers you left at the side of the bed. Gently tapping the floor with your toes from left to right, they are where you left them, only it is on the opposite side of the bed. You place your uncovered foot on the cold ceramic tile floor and receive the startling sensation of the cold room temperature. You slowly drag your limp body with partially closed eyes to the bath room and turn on the faucet and splash the refreshing water onto your face and a soothing comfort of awakening rushes over your body. You ready yourself for the morning trek to work to earn your daily bread. You prepare a quick light breakfast, make a small pot of coffee and listen to a portion of the morning news. You murmur how there is nothing but bad news every morning. When will those people ever show good news in the morning? Have to wake up to tragedy every morning! With that being said you change the channel. Oh my goodness! Look at the time; Time is passing fast this morning you say as you pick up the pace and rush to get dressed. You had the alarm set forty-five minute early before you had to leave your residence. You got up at the first sound of the alarm and did not hit the snooze button. You lounged around the house until the very last minute. Without regards to the surprise awaiting you outside, time has elapsed and you must leave. You did not give yourself any extra time for the unforeseeable. You are fully aware of the possibility that something may happen while in route to work or school, to an employment interview, doctor's appointment etc: You can encounter vehicle breakdowns, accidents, road work that snarl traffic and relegate you to move along at a snail pace. It seems these things may occur only when you are pressed for time. Now you are pressed for time.

You charge out the door trying to put your arm in the other sleeve of your coat and close the door simultaneously. The briskness of the cool air makes you hurry your pace. The sun is rising and it is cold out as you leave the comfort of your warm house. The most noticeable thing at first light is the thin sheet of ice on your windshield as the rays of the sun reflect its brightness back to the sky. You sat lounging around the house a little longer then usual catching the last of the news, watching your favorite morning program, pressing clothes, putting on make-up or getting the kids ready and now time is no longer on your side.

Exceptions can be made when you are coping with small children. Everyone who has had a couple school aged children four years or less apart understands.

You unlock the driver's side door and get inside your vehicle that's colder then the air outside. You turn the key to the ignition and start the engine, turn the defroster on full blast and began waiting impatiently for the windshield to defrost. You check your watch for the time only to discover you are now five minutes behind schedule and the windshield has not yet fully defrosted. It takes too long to thaw the windshield. You remember your friend from work telling you to put water on the windshield to help the windshield defrost quicker. You get out the car and get the garden hose to expedite the defrosting process. To your amazement it works! Well, you thought it did. Once you get back into the vehicle you realized it did not work to the fullest extent needed to be able to move the car. You are still unable to see through the windshield. Damn you say! You're going to be late! Your supervisor has already spoken to you regarding making it to work on time consistently. Maybe she was not talking directly to you when she addressed the entire group during the weekly meeting. But you were late one day of the week the entire month and you can't blame your tardiness on children the way other co-workers can. You have no children!

Without regard or clear vision you have to get going. You're already more then five minutes behind schedule. Barely able to peer through the small peephole that defrosted at the bottom of the windshield but it's enough for you to get going. You carefully pull out the driveway narrowly missing the three foot deep drainage ditch in front of your property. And you think you can drive! You cautiously approach the corner. You cannot see out the side glass because there is too much ice and frost on the windows. You never thought to lower the window for a better view, besides you don't want to let any more cold winter weather inside the vehicle. You strain to see through the small envelope size spot in the window where defrosting has begun. You make your move onto the main street. Suddenly, you are startled by the blaring of a car horn and you accelerate. You look into the rear view mirror and without clear vision you notice they were not as close as they were making it out to be and you call the driver a few choice words because the idiot is just like you. "They Think They Can Drive" but did not have on any lights to illuminate their vehicle at the break of dawn. At such an early time in the morning they should have on running lights at least to make it possible for you to see them through your frosted windows that you did not have time to thoroughly defrost. They should have their lights on you exclaim to yourself. You make yourself feel better with that thought. But if you could drive you would have left the interior of your comfortable residence sooner and given yourself time to properly thaw the windshield. Making correct decisions in the preparations of driving are without a doubt a part of good driving.

You have driven approximately a quarter mile and there is enough heat inside the vehicle that the windshield has cleared. You make your last turn before you approach the interstate in route to earn your daily bread. The turn signal was neglected! You make your final approach to the interstate and you notice there are a lot of drivers that like yourself Think They Can Drive.

There is this big foursquare yellow sign with black markings on it to indicate there are vehicle approaching the lane to enter onto the interstate. They are strategically placed along the interstate system near on and off ramps to advise motorist of approaching road conditions, it is universally known as a Merge Sign. Which means you should change lanes to not impede the flow of traffic as vehicles are merging onto the interstate system. But those drivers just as you Think They Can Drive also and ignore the meaning of the Merge Sign. They do not change lanes and does not increase speed or decrease speed to make it easier for you to access the highway system. Surely you have witnessed a few near misses? You may have even been involved in a few near misses as well as you tried to merge onto the interstate because you don't know how to utilize your turn signals and they don't know when to merge.

Not using any turn signals you manage to squeeze in the front of the driver like yourself who Think They Can Drive. They lean on their horn and call you a few dirty names, you blankity blank, blank. Talk about your mother and all your children. But evidently they are not aware of the courtesy of merging into another lane to let drivers enter onto the highway. Sure they think they can drive yet they do not respect the rules of the road. It's not that drivers don't know the rules of the roads. Some drivers don't think the rules apply to them. Or maybe they think their vehicle insurance will cover their accident problems. Who knows what s on the minds of some careless vehicle operators? They can be saddled with strife from a personal problem that makes it barely possible to think of the driving conditions.

They hurriedly jump from behind you, speed up to get on side of you and give you a stare (but you never look in their direction) they speed by you to show their disgust with your bad driving habits and put their bad driving habits on display by jumping directly in front of your vehicle with only inches to spare. They curse you and call you an idiot. But what is needed is a video to be given to them so they can see how idiotic they were when their patience was tested and temporarily lost control of good driving habits. But that don't matter, they were just venting to themselves and they wanted you to know they did not appreciate you jumping in front of them without utilizing your turn signals to request permission to enter the interstate. If they knew how to drive it would never had arrived at that situation. They would have merged into another lane and you would have had free access to the lane to enter the interstate whether you utilized your turn signal or not.

Now you are trying to do something no other driver is capable of doing while in rush hour traffic. You are going to make up for lost time and get back on schedule. You are determined to close the five minute time gap. The speed limit is posted at seventy miles per hour and you are going eighty. The average drivers who have given themselves enough time are traveling the posted speed limit and some of them are traveling five miles over the posted speed limit.

You leave out the designated slow lane and without using your turn signals make a dash for the center lane. The vehicle you cut in front of was a half car length behind you and you knew you had enough room. Which you did but you could have notified the driver of your intentions of wanting to get in front of them by using your turn signal. Since you did not and the driver was not expecting such a maneuver they had to hit their breaks harder which made the vehicle behind them brake a little harder to prevent from hitting the vehicle in front of them and it all reverts back to YOU!! Think You Can Drive. If you could drive, a lot of the miscalculation among the other drivers would not have occurred. Had you utilized the strength in your left index finger (assuming you have two hands) to activate the turn signal lever the driver would have slowed their pace to allow you room to change lanes and notify the driver behind them that a change in speed was necessary and the driver behind them would slow their pace and the near collision would never had occurred. The blood pressure of the other drivers would not have been raised to a new level. The levels where their eyes bulge out, they grab the steering wheel tightly embracing for impact and all the muscles in your body tense up. Yes! They too had a few choice words for you.

You hit the accelerator and increase your speed to catch up with the vehicle that is five car lengths in front of you. As you approach you do not ease up on the accelerator and began tailgating. The driver in front of you tap slightly on their brakes to make you back off. You comply momentarily and resume your tailgating exercise. You have an opening on your right and you have to make up for lost time. You dart out the fast lane into the center lane only to be behind slower traffic. You continue to move over to the far right lane. You accelerate past the car in the middle lane and cut in front of them only to find there is no way to increase your speed and maintain a consistent pace. You look to your left and now you are being passed by the driver you jumped in front of five vehicles back. Not only is that vehicle passing you but there is another ten cars you were once in front of now passing. You went from right lane to middle lane to left lane. Then from left lane to middle to right lane and back to middle lane and did not get any further than all the drivers maintaining a consistent speed. You have not gained any additional time, the only thing you did was raise your anxiety level along with the heighten anxiety level of a few other drivers. Reality of you being late has been accepted by you and you began to settle down, relax, listen to the music on the radio and drive accordingly. When you arrive at work and questioned by your supervisor as to why you are late you will tell your supervisor part of the truth and hope it is accepted. The part of the truth you will offer is the traffic was bad. You will exclude the part where you were home relaxing watching the early morning addition of the news and enjoying a good cup of coffee before preparing to leave for work.

Making good decisions behind the wheel of a lethal weapon indicates how well of a driver you are. You should not place yourself or others in danger because you don't know how to drive. Would you rather get to work late or get to heaven on time? Taking a few extra minutes to make certain your vehicle is road ready is the sign of good driving habits and the mark of a good driver. There's more to being a good driver then keeping the vehicle between the white lines. You do it so often you forget there is a thought process that goes along with driving. The computer between your ears has to be operational at all times, especially when you are behind the wheel of a deadly weapon. Surely statistics would provide factual information where you can label motor vehicles as deadly weapons. You utilize your computer so often while driving; everything becomes instinctive. All the darting in and out, the utilization of turn signals (when you use them), engaging and disengaging the brake, when to accelerate, when not to accelerate, you perform all these operations and more without thought while driving on the Interstates Highways. You have a thought to make a lane change, you look in the side mirror and you look in the rear view mirror to see if any vehicles are there to prevent you from making the lane change. You don't think should I use my turn signals for safety purpose. You instinctively hit the signal switch to indicate you are making a lane change. Other motorists choose not to signal when they perform the maneuver because no thought had to be given to the action and their instinct switch was turned off.

Sometimes your computer has to be re-booted by law enforcement. You get a re-boot when you are traveling at excessive speed and receive a citation from an officer of the law. You learn to slow down if not all the time at least some of the time. You get a re-boot when you are involved in an accident or near accident. It does not matter the severity. Once you are involved in an accident or near accident you change your driving habits. You no longer tail gate vehicles, knowing they can come to a sudden stop. You are more observant of other drivers, you slow your rate of speed and you utilize your turn signals more often. This is most often the reaction when the computer you have between your ears has been re-booted as a result of an accident, near accident or citation. You receive a re-boot when you are handed a citation from a law enforcement officer for driving at night without operational taillights. You moan and groan about having to pay for something you knew was not operational before you were stopped. Now you have to pay the city, county or state your hard earned money and still pay to have the vehicle made road worthy. In this case, an ounce of prevention (vehicle maintenance) would have been worth more than a pound of cure (paying the city, county or state).

It's indicative of a good driver to make sure all lights are operational, head lights, turn signals, brake lights and tail lights. Making certain all your safety equipment is operational is a sign of a good driver. Yes! One light can operate without the other being operational but someone who knows how to drive knows to make certain all their safety equipment is operational not just functional. A good driver checks all lights for safety. During inclement weather and it is "raining cat and dogs" an old adage used to describe how hard it's raining but never saw a cat or a dog fall from the sky. But you understand how bad the weather is and how hard the rain is coming down. Do you utilize your headlights to make your vehicle more visible from the front and rear? Do you turn on your headlights in foggy / rainy weather, how about when it is snowing? Do you turn on any lights when the driving conditions deteriorate to a point where visibility is 50% or less? Do you utilize your turn signals in such weather? This is definitely the time to use them if you don't normally use your turn signals. Surely you would want to be seen by other motorist as they would want to see you and be seen by you. How often have you witnessed drivers without their headlights and taillights on during inclement weather conditions creating a hazardous condition? Not only do they disregard utilizing their lights, they are traveling at a rate of speed (the speed limit) passing everyone as usual, because now all other responsible motorist are driving below the speed limit due to the weather. You do not see them until the last moment but thankfully they were seen. Yet, You think you can drive!

Driving on icy roads is much more hazardous than driving during a rain storm. Decreasing your speed does not necessarily help on icy roads but not decreasing your speed will cause major problems for everyone on the road. If you hit a patch of ice there is nothing you can do to control your vehicle. You hear the sounds of vehicles crashing into each other all around you and you see your vehicle sliding out of control toward the pile up. You turn the steering wheel to the left you turn the steering wheel to the right you tap your brakes in rapid succession. There is no response! You have lost control of steering way. Your vehicle is sliding in whatever direction the wind is blowing. You feel like performing a superman stunt and jumping out the vehicle to grab hold of the bumper and bring your car to a stop but all you can do is sit and brace for impact.

When you see a driver utilizing his lights, turn signals, maintaining a safe distance between the vehicles ahead of them and slowing their rate of speed during bad weather conditions you may think that driver may Know How to Drive.

Utilizing Turn Signals

How often do you utilize your turn signals? "You Think You Can Drive" how about a little self observation. You utilize your turn signals every time you make a lane change? You use them every time you are entering or exiting the interstate? Do you use them when you are making a turn at a signal light? You utilize them every time you are making a lane change to get in front of another motorist to let them know your intentions to change lanes? You utilize them when you are the last vehicle in the turn lane and the lane is backed up beyond the turn lane. You do this to notify on coming motorist the traffic is backed up in the turn lane. No, well maybe you should, it would allow the approaching driver who's not turning time to make a lane change and prevent traffic from coming to a complete stop and it may also prevent an accident. You often see debris (bumpers, finders, broken headlights and tail lights) on the side the road where an accident had occurred in the turning lane. There is a strong possibility the last vehicle in the turning lane did not have operational turn signals and brake lights were malfunctioning and the approaching driver was unable to compensate. By the time it was realized the vehicle up front did not have any functioning lights, time and distance to stop had passed and the accident became inevitable.

You should utilize your signals especially when you are making a lane change and there is a vehicle within two car lengths behind or in front of your vehicle. If you can let the other driver be aware that you will be making a maneuver to the other lane you may find your driving experience more comfortable and less tense. How often have you jumped in the front of another driver without utilizing your turn signals and you were only a few feet in front of the other motorist. You can't imagine how many vulgar names that person just called you. Maybe you can because you have called someone the very same when they cut you off without notice. They talked about you and your whole family. If you would have hit my new car you blankity, blankity, blank. It matters not to you; they are just upset they can't drive as well as you. So what they had to slam on their brakes and were almost rear-ended by someone else caught in the chain reaction of events you caused. Unless you are physically handicapped (no left arm) there really isn't a reason to not use your turn signals. The car manufactures did a wonderful thing by placing your turn signal switch only a matter of inches from your left hand. If your left hand is on the steering wheel (that's the big round thing you use to turn the vehicle) your finger will touch the signal switch automatically. They even had the audacity to make it move at the slightest touch. You don't have to be a weight lifter, you don't have to be a martial arts expert, there's nothing strenuous about it at all. A one year old love turning the switch off and on (when the vehicle is in park and the engine not running): and if they are not careful they will break it all the way off. Surely you have the strength of an infant. Why is it so difficult for you to utilize your turn signal when making a lane change? Do you think you will not be able to change lanes if you inform the other driver of your intentions to change lanes? Unlike you, some individuals can drive and they are not in a hurry like yourself and they will allow you to get two seconds ahead of them. The question is raised once again, how often do you utilize your turn signals and do you know when to use your turn signals?

You can't expect the interstate race car driver who passed you and everyone on the interstate darting from lane to lane to utilize something he don't have, remember race cars are not equipped with such luxuries. They feel the need for speed not the need for safety. They will slice in front of you within inches of your front bumper and don't care not even a little of how close he was to your vehicle. He is sure you will not get too close to his vehicle because you are a normal driver not a thrill seeking adrenalin junkie like them. Left lane, middle lane, right lane, in and out, faster and faster sometimes utilizing turn signals, sometimes not until they are out of site. You see them and think they can handle their vehicle pretty darn good which most of them can but they are careless and create anxieties within other drivers. The need for speed is gender neutral there is an equal amount of females experiencing adrenalin rushes. Female drivers has also transformed into Interstate Race Car drivers. They will pass you by like they are in the final stage of the last trimester and has to get to the hospital right now. Adrenalin rush is also flowing in the veins of the older more mature drivers. Not as much! But sometimes they get a boost and become Interstate Race Car drivers and start passing everything on the road. But that may happen mainly during emergencies.

Some Interstate Race Car drivers utilize their turn signals once out every three lane changes and some don't use them at all.

We can all be thankful motorists don't have to manually turn on a switch to operate the brake lights like they have to manually operate the turn signals. You may never know when the vehicle in the front of you is preparing to stop. Can you comprehend the destruction on the streets and highways if you had to depend on other motorist to manually turn on their brake lights "unimaginable chaos" especially during inclement weather if they would operate their brake lights as often as their turn signals.

Thank you car manufactures for the wonderful system design to use your feet instead of your hands to operate the brake lighting system.

Rush Hour

It is not just you whom think they can drive on a busy rush hour morning. As you look around you there are numerous individuals changing lanes too close to the vehicle they are getting ahead of without utilizing any signals. What would it hurt to inform the other driver of your intentions to change lanes? Are you afraid they will not let you get two seconds ahead of them? It only equates to approximately two seconds of time they would be behind you if they are courteous enough to allow you in front of them. But they may be in a similar position as you "late for work". They may not want to allow you to get in front of them even if you ask permission with your turn signals. Maybe they were out of position to allow you the distance to get ahead of them. In the event they do not comply and allow you to get ahead of them. Rest assured the next driver will because they had time to see you requesting permission with your turn signal.

Notice that maybe one out of five drivers utilizes their turn signals consistently? Those who do not will jet in between you and the vehicle ahead of you and never consider providing you with a courtesy warning. Any type of courtesy blank of the turn signal to inform you they are changing lanes or would like to get in front of your vehicle would be helpful. You would have time to adjust your speed to allow space between the two of you and it would also prevent you from having to suddenly hit your brakes creating a domino effect with other motorist slamming their brakes to prevent accidents. When you have to suddenly slam your brakes the vehicles behind you do the same thing. Now everyone's pressure has increased a couple notches in that instance. Some of them used a few choice words to express their sentiment. After a few seconds your blood pressure return to normal and you continue on your destiny.

In a Hurry to Go Nowhere

It is possible a lot of morning and afternoon congestion can be prevented if motorist truly knew how to drive and put patience in the passenger seat. Everyone is in a hurry to go nowhere. Where ever it is you are trying to go, it will be there if you get there or not. This does not apply to trying to catch alternative modes of transportation, (airplanes, trains, buses or ships) they very well may not be there when you get there. Unlike you they may be on schedule.

How often have you been passed by a driver exceeding the speed limit by more then ten miles an hour above the limit you are traveling and you are traveling five miles above the posted speed limit yourself. The irony is you will more then likely catch up with them in less than a minute during rush hour traffic. Try this! Next time someone passes you like they are trying to catch a cheating spouse. Observe their license plate number or the vehicle itself if it stands out and look at your watch. Check to see how long it will take to catch up to the driver that passed you in a hurry during rush hour traffic. When traffic is moving at the same rate of speed you will catch up to them in a minute or two. The exception; if you are passed by someone who thinks they are at Teladago. They are weaving in and out of traffic like they want to be the first across the finish line. Oh yea! They won't be utilizing any turn signals. Racing vehicles don't come equipped with them. Besides the boss informed them if they arrive at work tardy one more time they will have to seek employment elsewhere. You will not catch them!! They are trying to beat time. They have fifteen minutes to get to work park their car and hit the clock on time. Trouble is they are twenty minutes from work. Now they are trying to accomplish something no scientist has yet proven can be done. "Catch Time" Once the elusive time has passed you can not at any rate of speed catch up. Unless you are traveling at the speed of time! The one minute you are behind can never be recaptured. It's gone it's the past you are just racing into the future. May as well slow down and rejoin everyone in the present. Where ever you are rushing to get to will be there when you arrive. It's best to be late at the golden gate than to get in hell on time.

If you are driving behind a vehicle and you find yourself braking often to slow your vehicle, the vehicle in the front of you may be going too slow but the fact is you are going too fast. Have you ever experienced driving behind a vehicle engaging their brake pedal frequently every few seconds? You are unsure of what is taking place ahead of them only to discover they were riding the rear bumper of the vehicle directly in front of them. Brake light after brake light but you are driving a safe distance behind the vehicle directly in front of you and you never had to brake just let up on the gas pedal a little. Try slowing to a speed that will create a distance of two car lengths between you and the vehicle in front of you and it is guaranteed you will not have to engage your brakes as often. "Be patient" wherever you are rushing to will be there when you get there if not catch the next one. Who knows? The life you save may be your own. And when someone cuts in the front of the vehicle ahead of you making them slam their brakes you will have enough time to brake or change lanes if necessary.

The person trying to make up time will never be more then sixty seconds in front of the first vehicle they cut in front of anyway. It has something to do with mathematics and physic, time traveled and distance traveled and when you toss in average speed, everyone will reach the same destination at approximately the same time when traveling toward an identical vicinity, even the person traveling eighty miles per hour during rush hour traffic. Once they exit the interstate highway they will always be stopped by something. A red light, stop sign, road work, school bus something will require them to reduce speed and you will find yourself directly behind them occasionally walking in the building or plant simultaneously.

One of the more intriguing sights to witness is to see an impatient motorist thinking he was on an international speedway and not the interstate highway, emotionally feeling every driver ahead of him was not traveling at a fast enough speed to satisfy the adrenalin rush racing through his veins. Although most are traveling at or maintaining the posted speed limit of seventy miles per hour, others motorist are traveling five to ten mile an hour over the speed limit. Traffic is fairly congested but moving at a steady pace.

There are areas of the interstate that has three lanes. This is generally true when you are traveling within the city limits. On the out skirts of the city (rural areas) the interstate is two lanes.

But on a three lane interstate highway within the city limits there's also an emergency lane. It should be used for just what the name implies "emergencies" if a vehicle breaks down or becomes disabled it is there for their safety and the safety of all motorist on the highway. It is not for the impatient high adrenalin junky to utilize at their discretion. Because they do not want to follow the rules of the road they jeopardize the safety of other motorist. Traveling in the slow lane of traffic on the right hand side of the interstate and exceeding the posted limit by three miles an hour when something catches your attention through your rear view mirror. And you see Joe Impatient approaching at a speed greater than you are traveling and you think he better slow down and at that moment he moves to the emergency lane and began passing on the shoulder of the road. He's driving like someone trying to catch a cheating spouse. He has total disregard for all other motorist on the highway. You can tell other motorist ahead of you noticed what he was doing and began to tighten the gaps between vehicles and he was unable to get back onto the highway. The traffic was rapidly approaching an obstacle in the emergency lane. Joe Impatient saw the obstacle approaching and decides he was going to now be courteous and ask someone permission to let him back onto the highway and he turns his signal light on. Now he wants someone to be considerate of his request and ignore his bad driving behavior and his disregard for the safety of others. No one complied with his request and no one slowed down to provide access and all vehicles in the front and pulling up the rear would not let Joe Impatient gain access back onto the interstate. That obstacle was a small bridge over a small body of water. Joe Impatient had run out of road and had to come to a complete stop and was not able to get back onto the highway until he could no longer be seen through the rear view mirror. Sometime it is comforting to witness those who think they can drive not get away with every bad driving maneuver they choose. It feels even better when you witness them getting caught by law enforcement.

Traffic is at a standstill as an accident up ahead is being processed and here come Jane Impatient making her move in the emergency lane because she has to get to where she has to get to. Must be a going out of business shoe sale at Macy's, well Jane Impatient did not see Mr. State Trooper when he pulled out behind her. Maybe she did! Especially when the lights came on, although she was in a hurry to go nowhere it will take her that much longer to get there and her bank account will be a little lighter. Was she rushing to get to the hospital? Whomever it is in the hospital that she is rushing to see is being taken care of by the medical staff and there is nothing you will be able to do if you do get there in a hurry. If it's that kind of an emergency chances are they will not allow you to visit until they have stabilized the person you are rushing to see. The best you will do is wait in the waiting area with all the other anxiety filled, concerned family and friends. You could have save yourself some money by being more patient under stressful conditions and not drove in the emergency lane. The State Trooper that writes the citation will not sympathize with your emergency alibi. He listens to them all day long. There's only a few exceptions to what a State Trooper accept to be bonafied emergencies and you being late for work is not one of them.

WOMEN, &
ELDERLY DRIVERS

Once upon a time females and the elderly were the meek of the roadways. Not so long ago, in the not so distant past both groups were the most courteous and cautious drivers on the roads. Ladies would be traveling with their children in vehicles on road trips, going to school, taking a trip to the relatives or traveling to the market and they would utilize the utmost caution with their children on board. This being a time prior to the existing restraint laws across the nation and mobile communication was non-existent. Ladies of times pasted would have their children safely locked into the seat belts. They drove in the right lane and maintained the posted speed, in most cases they were traveling below the limit. "Safe and cautious"

The elderly seemed to only drive on their way to the doctor's office or heading to church. It matter not where they would be traveling their speed was a constant slow. Neither of the groups would exceed the posted speed limit and they would generally maintain their speed in the right lane. Not too often "(in the not so distant past)" would the speed limit be broken by any member of these two groups. They drove with caution and care, law enforcement agencies archived records could provides the necessary verification. Citations for females and elderly once researched would probably be at a minimum as it pertains to speeding and reckless driving.

That was the not so distant past: fast forward from the seventies, eighties and nineties and today's new millennium female and elderly drivers have come a long way baby. Females are just as likely to pass you at fifteen mile per hour faster than any man on the highway. They no longer have a fear of speed. Matter of fact, they feel the need for speed. The thrill seeker within is no longer contained. The thrill seeker is out and they are flaunting it. They are flaunting it without caution and they are not courteous. How often have you been passed by a young mother with an infant strapped in the child seat? How often have you witnessed the careless operation of their vehicle with a child on board? Traveling at speeds up to ten mph greater than the posted speed limit and changing lanes with less than a car length between them and the car they cut in front of and of course, they do not use turn signals. They have one hand on the steering wheel and the other on the phone surely you can't expect them to utilize turn signals. Or they thrill seekers or just plain bad careless drivers?

The driving habits for the elders has changed also, being passed by the Geritol generation has become common everyday occurrences. Today's retirees are on the go. No more sitting at home letting life past them by waiting on time to relieve them of existence. They too want to enjoy all aspects of life and thrill seeking on the interstate is a good way to safely seek thrills. Seventies are the new sixties, so they say. How often have you been passed on the highway by someone of the retirement age traveling at the speed of Geritol. Yea! They have some get up and go, no more driving like its Sunday morning or cruising to a doctor's appointment, seventy is the new sixty. The elders have places to go, people to meet, things to do beep, beep move over and let them through. The elders are no longer contained by what you are supposed to do at a certain age. The rules have changed for elders as times have changed for all drivers. What was once expected of that age group when it comes to driving no longer exist. In times past it was expected the elderly would drive in the right lane only (the slow lane) but since the invention of the contact lenses and they don't have to wear bifocals. The elders feel a need for speed. They can focus on the driving lanes more clearly and passing you at ten mph greater than the posted limit is very thrilling. When you look at them they look at you and smile.

Have you been driving in the center lane recently on an Interstate Highway and looked to your left and saw a white haired grandmother or grandfather zoom by you at speeds exceeding the posted speed limit? Now you see them zoom by you on telephones. It's hard to ask if You Think You Can Drive to someone who may have been driving for forty years or more. Of course they think they can drive. But it's obvious they can't! It only means they have been doing it a long time.

You don't obey the rules of the road, you exceed the posted speed limits by more than ten miles an hour and some motorist has become so impatient they have resulted in passing other motorist utilizing the shoulder of the road and they think they can drive. The posted speed limit is seventy miles an hour you are traveling at a rate of speed five mile an hour greater than the posted limit, you look in your rear view mirror and see an approaching motorist getting closer and closer to your vehicle. You began wondering if they are going to slow down because they are approaching you so fast and they don't. They suddenly jump into the middle lane and accelerate to a rate much greater than the posted limits. It make you wonder how fast is fast enough? You exceed the limits by five miles an hour and you are passed by others at ten miles an hour above the limit. Now drivers are traveling at a speed of eighty-five miles an hour and guess what, they are being passed by others motorist exceeding even the eighty-five other are traveling. Everyone is in a hurry to go nowhere and they want to get there as quickly as possible.

COURTEOUS DRIVERS

Are you one of those drivers who think they are the honorary highway patrol? You know the motorist! They are the drivers who refuse to yield the right away when they are traveling at the posted speed limit in the fast lane. They are the driver that sees approaching traffic traveling at a rate of speed greater then what you are traveling. You are going to force them to slow down or go around. Some will flash their lights to let you know they want you to move over and others will tail gate you until you get out of their way. In your mind they should be obeying the posted speed limit. But you are not the one who should determine how fast someone else should be traveling. Leave speed adjustments to those that are being paid to control speed (Highway Patrols, State Troopers, Law Enforcement Officers in general) on the roadway. Only after you have been passed by several drivers where some angrily go around you and jump directly in front of you within a matter of feet between the two vehicles and curse you and your family will you submit and move to a slower lane.

You think you can drive but do you change lanes when approaching a police action on the side of the highway if you have the opportunity to merge to another lane? Do you give the patrolman the courtesy to show him/her you care about their safety? If you are unable to change lanes due to heavy traffic and you can't get over do you slow your rate of speed? When you look in your side view mirror and see a vehicle approaching at a higher rate of speed but far enough back that does not prevent you from changing lanes do you increase your speed when you change lanes not to impede their progress (utilizing turn signals) or do you maintain the same rate of speed when you changed lanes forcing the oncoming motorist to decelerate? You adjust your speed accordingly until you pass the area where the police action is taking place and return to the lane you were traveling in before merging without impeding the rate of speed of the approaching motorist.

There is always the possibility of something occurring that may force the officer to suddenly move away from the vehicle and step into oncoming traffic. Who knows, maybe a vicious dog jump toward the window and the officer instinctively jump back into the traffic. Would you have time to stop? Change lanes when possible or slow down. Truck drivers are good at showing that type of courtesy. They will merge lanes when Law Enforcement Officers or Mr. and Mrs. Motorist are on the shoulder of the highway. If they pass to close to someone on the shoulder of the road "who knows" the tail wind from the truck may suck them up in the back draft. You may know someone too light in the rear where a strong wind can blow them away.

There are motorist that can drive and they prove it every time they get inside their vehicles. They perform periodic safety checks on their vehicles to ensure everything is operational they utilize turn signals when making a maneuver on the interstate, changing lanes. They utilize signals when entering or exiting the roadway. Good drivers merge to another lane when approaching merging traffic to not impede motorist getting onto the interstate system. They merge to another lane when they see an officer of the law on the side of the road performing his/her duties to keep the highway safe. Good drivers don't exceed the posted speed limit during inclement weather and turn on their lights when visibility has decreased. Good drivers slow their rate of speed when it is raining with the knowledge that if they had to come to a sudden stop maintaining control of a vehicle can be very difficult on a wet slippery road surface. Good drivers travel at speeds of five to ten mph under the limit during rainy and foggy weather. They will decrease their speed lower depending on the severity of the weather conditions. Good drivers maintain a distance of two car lengths behind the nearest vehicle giving them self time to maneuver if something occurs within their field of view. There are numerous motorists that not only Think They Can Drive, They Can! What about you?

About the Author

E. M. Williams, born under the zodiac sign Sagittarius in 1955, places strong emphasis on spiritual well being, faith and love.